How to CoParent During the Holidays

Tips for CoParenting Success and Reducing Stress

Diane Windsor

www.MotinaBooks.com

We publish books by mothers, and for mothers.

Other Books by Diane Windsor:

Smoke Screen

How to Relationship

Calming, Art Therapy Coloring Book for Single Moms

DEDICATION

This book is dedicated to all single parents.
You're doing a great job!!

Introduction

On a sweltering Texas night in August, my 24-year-old daughter and I were talking about jobs, boyfriends, and life. Her father and I divorced when she was only one and a half. She told me that as she was growing up she never felt that her dad and I forced her to choose between us. She wasn't placed in the middle of arguments.

We didn't even make her go to a different house on the weekends; my ex and I lived in the same neighborhood, and her home base was with him. I talked to my girl every day and saw her most days, but her home was with her father.

My ex and I really worked on doing what was best for our kids. This is the key—even though you and your ex aren't together anymore, if you put the best interests of your children first, if you make them your number one priority, everyone will be okay.

Try to keep this in mind as you prepare for the holidays.

This book is designed to help single parents cope with the stress that the holiday season can bring in several ways.

First, our goal is to provide you with advice that can help you and your ex coparent successfully during the holiday season. This means keeping the best interests of the kids at the forefront. I know that you both want to be with your children. Just keep in mind that their needs are the most important thing. And, at this time of year, their wants should be considered as well.

After each chapter you'll find several note pages where can record your thoughts and feelings. What are you doing during the holidays, either with or without your children? What are you happy or sad about?

What are your goals and dreams?

If you're a list-maker, like I am, you could use these pages to record the things you need to do, and stay organized.

Finally, throughout this book you'll find beautiful mandalas for you to color. Coloring has becoming a very popular activity, specifically for reducing stress, and instilling calmness.

I hope you enjoy this book, and that it provides you with some valuable information, and some peace.

It's ok for me to think about my own goals and dreams.

Write down some of your goals and dreams.

Togetherness

The Holiday Season is all about family togetherness. School's out for a couple of weeks, and many people take time off from work, just to spend time with those they love. No matter which holiday you celebrate at the end of the year, there's a special feeling in the air; it's magical.

But if you're a single parent, especially a newly divorced or separated single parent, the holidays can be a very sad, stressful time of year. The time that, in the past, you've so looked forward to has become a time spent arguing about visitation, and missing your kids.

As the leader of a large single parent support group, and a former single parent, I'm very familiar with the frustration and loneliness that many single parents experience this time of year. My ex-husband lived in a different state. Christmas vacation was one of the few times during the year that my son was able to spend some time with his father.

I'll never forget that first year, when I needed to put

my eight-year-old on an airplane all by himself. Believe me, that was NOT easy! The UM's (Unaccompanied Minors) were allowed to board the plane first. My little guy had a lanyard around his neck with a badge that contained his name, my name, and his dad's name. No one would hand him over to his dad until credentials were checked and double-checked.

The flight attendants were always so kind and helpful. I was allowed to accompany him to the gate, because of his UM status. We waited together quietly at the gate. Then, the call for "pre-boarding" was announced. After I gave him a great big hug, and made sure I didn't start crying right in front of him, they took him down the jet way. I knew they would help him find his seat, and offer him a drink and a snack right away.

I continued to wait at the gate, while the rest of the passengers boarded. Parents of UM's were asked to stay until the plane was on its way. I sat there on that vinyl seat, halfway hoping that he'd come running out the door, back to me, and throw himself into my arms.

"I don't want to go, Mommy," he would say. "I want to stay with you."

But that was my own selfish wish. I knew that wasn't what he wanted, and that wouldn't be what was best for him. He was excited for his first plane ride, all by himself! It was all he had talked about for a week. And he loved his dad with all his heart, and missed him terribly. I really hoped that this time together would give the two of them a chance to reconnect, and make some wonderful memories together.

There is no one right way to coparent, or even to

parent. Everyone needs to figure out what works best for their family. And, you and your ex are in some ways still a family. You will always be part of each other's lives because of your child.

I'm the leader of a large single parent group in North Texas. I interact with many single parents, and I hear all kinds of stories about how difficult it can be to work with the "other" parent. This can be especially true around the holidays. Emotions are high—everyone wants to spend time with the children, including grandparents and other extended family members. We all understand this; children are what the holidays are all about!

In this book I'll address common issues that affect divorced parents and their children. These issues are present throughout the year, but may be magnified during holidays and vacation times.

I want all of you—you, your ex, your children, and all of your friends and extended family, to enjoy a peaceful, lovely holiday season.

It is possible!

Visitation Orders

I remember meeting Jen at one of our regular single parent get-togethers. There were about twelve attendees that night, and we were having a lively conversation about legal issues that most commonly affect single parents. You know, child support and visitation; those topics. It was our October meeting, so the holiday season was right around the corner.

The meeting ended, and people were filing out the door. A few stayed a little longer, catching up with each other and sharing their experiences. I noticed that a woman named Jen was still sitting quietly in her seat. She had been pretty quiet during our meeting; I wondered if her questions had been answered by some of the conversations that had taken place, or if she still wanted to talk. I sat down next to her, and she told me her story.

Jen was newly divorced, with a nine-year-old daughter. When a divorce is new that is the most difficult time. It can take quite a while before parents figure out how to work together. Jen was still trying to figure that out.

She explained to me that the visitation agreement stipulated that each parent would be able to spend their birthdays with their daughter. It also stipulated that visitation for each parent during the Christmas holidays would alternate each year.

That sounds like a reasonable arrangement right? Well, Jen didn't think so. Her birthday is on Christmas Day and she expected to spend that day with her daughter every year. She was not asking for the entire day as long as she could have a few hours with her daughter. Now remember, the divorce was still very new and they were still working out the kinks. Emotions were still high.

Jen's ex-husband's family lives in another state. It was easier for him to travel to see all of them, than for that entire extended family to pack up and visit him. So, understandably, he really wanted to take his daughter to visit her grandparents, aunts, and uncles. It was during the school break, so there was no worry that she would be missing school.

But Jen could not imagine spending her birthday without her daughter. That was the only gift she wanted, and she really felt that she deserved it! After all, that's what it said in the Visitation Orders, right?

The idea of being alone on both her birthday and Christmas terrified Jen. What had traditionally been a day of celebration and family, was certainly going to be depressing and lonely. Jen had every right to insist that her daughter not go out of town to visit her grandparents. It said so right there in black and white!

Let's imagine what could potentially happen if Jen were to insist on having it her way. Her ex-husband would visit his family without his daughter. Now, Jen did tell me that her daughter wanted to go. She didn't get to see her grandparents very often, and it had been a long time since she had been on a fun adventure to another state. There was also the promise of snow, which is not very common in her North Texas home.

But, unfortunately, Jen wasn't really thinking about what her daughter wanted. She was focusing on what she wanted, and what she felt she deserved. Again, it's what was ordered by the Court. So, Jen's daughter ends up staying at home with her mom. Jen does her best to make the time they spend together fun; they go to movies, out to dinner, and even allows one of her daughter's friends to spend the night.

They spend some real quality time together. But, Jen knows that her daughter would rather be with her dad. She simply isn't acting like herself; Jen can tell that she feels resentful. She's beginning to wish that she had handled the situation differently.

Jen could have given her permission for her daughter to visit her grandparents out of state, even though the Visitation Orders stated that it was her time. Even though it wasn't something that she wanted to do, she would know it's what is best for her daughter. Not only is she giving a gift to her daughter, she's also giving a gift to her ex-husband. This can be very difficult to do, especially when a divorce is new. But taking the high road can go a long way, and help contribute to a successful co-parenting relationship.

Just because the Visitation and Parenting Orders

specify the time that each parent spends with their child, it doesn't mean that you can't compromise sometimes. That's actually what the judges really like to see. They want parents to be able to work together and cooperate with each other. Talk to your ex about what is best for your child, and do your best to come to an agreement.

Taking the High Road is not easy. It's tough to be nice to someone when you would rather rip their face off. It's okay to start small. Write down a few easy, small ways that you can cruise down that High Road.

_____

_____

_____

_____

_____

_____

_____

_____

_____

Different Households,

Different Rules

Denise had a great question during one of our single parent get-togethers. She wanted to know what to do when you have one set of rules at your house, and your ex has another set of rules at his? This can be incredibly frustrating.

Is one parent right, and the other wrong? There are so many different ways to bring up a child. Even married parents can have a hard time agreeing on a parenting style. Dad might think it's totally fine to let the five-year-old watch action movies with loud explosions, while Mom thinks it's much too intense. Who's right in that situation? I know different people have different opinions. And that's okay! But it's helpful when both parents are on the same sheet of music when it comes to raising their kids.

Denise believes it's important to adhere to a strict bedtime schedule for her two children. She's found that it helps so much when they need to get up for school in the morning. She likes to stick to this schedule even on the weekends and during holidays. They are well-rested and happy when they wake up in the morning.

But, it isn't like this at Dad's house! Dad likes to have a party when the kids come over. They stay up late watching scary movies (which really gets Denise's goat) and eating junk food. The kids think it's great, of course. They love spending time with Dad.

And when the time comes for the kids to go back to Denise's house, they are more than happy to tell her how late they stayed up on Christmas Eve (it was after midnight!), the snacks they ate (a whole box of cookies!), and the movies they watched (*Polar Express* and *Krampus!*).

With each new story that she hears, Denise can feel her blood pressure rise. Her face is getting hot and she knows that she needs to act now! She grabs her phone and dials her ex's number. Before he can finish saying, "Hello," she starts lecturing him. She isn't letting him get a word in edgewise. All he hears is everything that he's doing wrong as a father. He feels that his ex-wife never has anything good to say to him, or about him. In his mind, he just wants to make the most out of the time that he has to spend with his children. It's never enough; he would love to see them more, but he knows he needs to follow the visitation orders. So, he just wants them to have fun when they're all together.

Denise is still lecturing him, her voice becoming louder and more agitated. Finally, he can't stand listening to her anymore, and he begins yelling back at her. This is a typical conversation after the kids have spent time with their dad. Now, everyone is upset, especially the kids.

How could this situation have been handled differently?

I know that when it comes to raising your kids, you have very strong opinions. I know that I did. I never wanted my children to touch a drop of soda – ever!

For the sake of everyone's sanity (you, your ex, and your kids) it's vital that you take a step back, and think about what is really important. You and your ex will be involved with each other for the rest of your lives. Do you think your relationship can end when the kids graduate from high school? That's not realistic. There will be weddings, grandchildren, and many other special moments that will be celebrated.

Do you want to be that person who says to your daughter, "If she's coming to the dinner celebrating your promotion to Vice President of Sales, then I won't be there."

Really? So, do you expect your child to hold two celebratory dinners? Or, do you really want your kiddo to choose between you and their other parent? Think about that for a moment. I know that the two of you don't get along very well. Your ex drives you up a tree, and the two of you can't agree on anything. That's probably a big part of why you're not together anymore.

But remember this—your children should not have to choose between the two of you. They're entitled to love both parents. Your children's lives will be better if their mom and dad are both involved with them, forever.

That said, let's return from our trip to the future. I know that when your ex allows the kids to do things that you don't like, like stay up late and eat junk food, it drives you nuts. But, you know it's not going to kill them. If your children are in potential danger at your ex's house, then you certainly need to take action and make sure nothing harmful happens to them. That's not what we're talking about in this situation. In this case, and many others, we're talking about different parenting styles, of which there is no right one. Opinions are like noses—everyone has one.

It will go a long way with your ex, if you can demonstrate that you respect his or her opinion. Compromise a little. You'll see that they'll start to compromise with you, too. I would recommend to Denise that when she talks to her ex about the kids, she tries very hard to stay in control, and to give him an opportunity to speak.

I also think she should let a few of these things go. If she says to her ex, "I know that the kids have a lot of fun with you, and I think that's great. I'm just a little worried about them watching a scary movie so late at night. Do you think you could skip that next time?"

Denise is bound to get a more cooperative response if she phrases her request like this.

One more thing; this conversation doesn't need to take place in front of the children. Please don't argue with their other parent within earshot of the kids. It doesn't do them any good. Remember—they are allowed to love both of you.

Make a list of the things your ex does that really bug you! Then, see if you can come up with a few ways that you can make a difference. Don't try to change your ex—work on changing your approach to the issues that bother you.

I hate it when when my ex...

_____

_____

_____

_____

_____

_____

_____

_____

_____

_____

_____

_____

_____

_____

I can try to make it better by.....

_____

_____

_____

_____

_____

_____

_____

_____

_____

_____

_____

_____

_____

_____

_____

_____

I hate it when when my ex...

I can try to make it better by.....

_____

_____

_____

_____

_____

_____

_____

_____

_____

_____

_____

_____

_____

_____

_____

Simple, Special Moments

The holiday season makes everyone crazy. The traffic, the crowds, the feeling that you'll never get everything done on time! Add to this the fact that many people typically overspend during the holidays, and it is not a very joyful season.

When I go shopping anywhere close to Christmas, even if it's just a trip to the grocery store, I consciously remind myself to be patient. I know that I'm going to have to deal with so many people, and everyone is harried. This is the time to take a deep breath, and realize that your task is probably going to take a bit longer than you had originally expected.

We want everything to be perfect; the gifts, the decorations, the food—everything! How many of you have boxes of decorations that you've had for years, probably dating back to your childhood? I know they'll be lovingly draped all over your home. You'll also probably crawl into the attic to haul down the inflatables and light-up reindeer that spend a couple of weeks on your lawn each year.

Or maybe you want to make homemade gifts for all of your friends and co-workers, like you did that one year before you had kids. STOP!!

One year, as a single mom with three kids in school, I decided that I was going to make homemade cranberry/strawberry jam for all of my co-workers. There were about 50 people working in that office, and I wanted to make sure that I had a jar of jam for every one of those people! I stayed up much too late for a week, measuring sugar, boiling jars, and hulling strawberries. I was a wreck!

Trying to fit the many holiday preparations into an already busy schedule can easily put you over the edge. It doesn't have to be this way; really. Experiencing a more simple, less stressful Christmas can be just as joyful.

Decorating

There was a time in my life when I strung lights along the outside of the house until it looked like the Griswold's home in Christmas Vacation. The icicles hung from the eaves, and each window was framed in twinkle lights. There were at least three inflatables in the front yard; my favorite was Santa on a motorcycle. And don't get me started with the trees! There was a live tree in the family room, an artificial one in the upstairs game room, and each of my kids had their own mini-tree. Of course, each tree had its own collection of themed and color coordinated decorations. It's safe to say that I went a teeny bit overboard when it came to decorating.

For several years after my divorce I kept up the tradition of mega-decorating. I thought it was what my kids wanted, and I wanted them to have a nice Christmas.

I'll never forget one morning when I was getting ready for work. Part of my routine was to make sure there was enough water in the container holding the Christmas tree. As I bent over to pour the water from a plastic measuring cup into the container, I noticed that something didn't seem quite right. The tree was leaning. I didn't think it had been like that the night before, but I didn't think much of it. That was a mistake. Almost as soon as I stood up, the tree came crashing down.

I jumped in front of it, trying to save it, but it was no use. The tree, the decorations, and water were all over the floor. I lost it. I burst into tears, staring at the mess on the family room floor.

My oldest son had heard the commotion, and walked into the room.

"Mom, why are you crying," he asked, as he began lifting the tree back into place.

"The whole tree just crashed down, and now it's a total mess!" I said through my tears.

"Mom, it's okay. It's just a tree."

Those four little words, "It's just a tree," hit me like a ton of bricks. It *was* just a tree. Why was I getting so upset about it?

Trying to have the perfect decorations was making me crazy. I was not able to function well at work and at home, and also put up an enormous amount of elaborate decorations.

That day, I decided to scale back dramatically. I didn't

need multiple large Christmas trees; one smallish one in the family room was plenty. We decorated it with our most cherished ornaments, not the color-coordinated ones. I also settled on one inflatable for the front yard, and minimal lighting. I really didn't like getting up on a high ladder, so it didn't take much convincing to make this change!

Cutting back on decorating allowed me to enjoy more time just being with my kids.

Activities

There are so many potential activities that you can attend during the holidays! Neighborhood parties, office parties, the Nutcracker, the tree lighting event in your town, your book club's cookie exchange, and so on, and so on.

Guess what!

You don't have to attend every Christmas party that you're invited to!

Pick and choose the events that are most important to you. If you really enjoy your neighborhood's Christmas potluck, then you should absolutely attend. Potlucks are typically fairly easy, because you only have to worry about preparing one dish.

If you're a baker, and you love the tradition of baking cookies with your children, consider preparing the cookie dough before you actually do the baking. Cookie dough keeps very well in the fridge for a couple of days, and the fun part is really cutting out the cookie shapes, and decorating them, right? Maybe one day if your kids are busy doing something else, you could prepare one or two different types of cookie dough. Then, when you're together with your kids, they can create the shapes, and eat some cookies right out of the oven.

Another simple, yet very fun, traditional activity is driving through neighborhoods and admiring other people's Christmas lights. We used to make this really fun, by bringing along hot chocolate and wearing our PJs. Yes, I would wear my Santa pajama pants and climb in the driver's seat.

We would drive around the neighborhoods in our town and admire all the lights that I didn't need to string up by myself.

Gifts

There would have been a time that I would have stayed up until 2:00 in the morning, making homemade gifts for all of my co-workers and friends. I have made fabric covered poofy photo albums and hand-painted wooden signs. It's taken a long time for me to realize that giving everyone a handmade (or expensive) gift is not necessary.

Many of us spend extra hours making gifts, thinking that we're saving money. But you know the truth, don't you? By the time you leave Michael's or Hobby Lobby, you've spent more in craft materials than you would have just buying some small, simple gifts!

One of the sweetest gifts I received from a co-worker was a little plate with a snowman on it, and a few cookies. I'm pretty sure she bought the plates at Walmart, so we know they weren't very expensive. The cookies may have been homemade, or they may have been store bought. It really didn't matter. It was a lovely way to be remembered.

There have been plenty of times when I've just given my co-workers a card. It's a lovely way of showing that you're thinking about someone, and wish them joy and happiness. If you absolutely have to make something, handmade cards are not a bad choice. This is an activity that kids would really enjoy, and they can give some of the cards to their friends.

I've found that quite often we end up making a memory when we didn't intend to. It happened the most when we were doing simple things together, like taking the dog for a walk. What your kids want the most is to be with you.

Traditions
to Keep

_____

_____

_____

_____

_____

_____

_____

_____

_____

_____

_____

_____

_____

_____

We can Ditch These!!

_____

_____

_____

_____

_____

_____

_____

_____

_____

_____

_____

_____

_____

_____

_____

_____

Celebrating Together

The first few years after a divorce occurs are the hardest. There are so many emotions on both sides, and often many hurt feelings. Both of you are trying to figure out how this new lifestyle is going to work. It's often difficult to be in the same room together, or have a civil conversation over the phone (or text).

In my experience, I have found that as time passes, the relationship between a divorced couple becomes a little easier. Where in the beginning there may have been animosity, that tends to fade over time. Now, I know that every situation is different, so please understand that this won't happen in every case. But usually, hard feelings will start to go away, and you might actually be able to stand each other.

Being able to celebrate special occasions as a family would be a wonderful gift to your children. For them to be able to see Mom and Dad getting along and being civil to each other, even if they can't live together, is a fantastic lesson.

There are many options for celebrating together. You certainly don't need to have a huge holiday dinner together, like you did when you were married. But spending some time together with your children and your ex will demonstrate to your children that you both are able to be kind to each other. This behavior will also give your kids permission that they do not need to choose a side, and are allowed to love both of you.

If emotions between you and your ex are still running a little high, but you'd like to take a crack at celebrating together, there are some options you can consider that will help make things go smoothly.

First, meet at a restaurant, or another location where you both feel comfortable. It isn't a good idea to meet at one of your homes. That would be sure to make one of you uneasy. You can all easily meet somewhere casual like a fast-food restaurant, ice cream parlor, or a park, if the weather is cooperating.

As we've already mentioned, it's extremely important that the kids understand that they have permission to love both parents. Children should never have to choose between the two of you, no matter how you feel about each other. Give your children a small budget to buy a gift for the other parent. Ideally, both Mom and Dad will do this and provide a little something for the other parent.

Of course, you can't control what the other parent does or doesn't do. Even if they do not come prepared with packages for you, you should still make a small effort. Show your kids that you can be kind.

As time goes by, and emotions are not as high as they are in the beginning, you may find that it's possible to celebrate holidays together in a new way.

What are some small ways that you, your ex, and your children can spend some time together as a family?

_____

_____

_____

_____

_____

_____

_____

_____

_____

_____

_____

_____

_____

_____

Avoid Financial Stress

Everyone feels the pinch during the holidays. Not only single parents, but families with two parents can easily overextend themselves when they're trying to fulfill everyone's wish list. It's so easy to overdo it and put all of your purchases on a credit card, without realizing how much you're spending. Then when the bill comes in January, it's shocking!

Many single parents fall into the trap of wanting to give their kiddoes a lot of gifts, in an effort to make up for the divorce. I remember a conversation I had years ago with another single parent. This was the time when I first started living on a budget, and I was really trying to be intentional with my money. I was working hard toward getting out of debt and setting up an emergency fund. During this process, I was also talking to my kids about money and teaching them about budgeting and saving.

I told another single mom about my plan to live on a

budget so I could get out of debt and start saving money. To my surprise, she started berating me for not buying more gifts for them!

"What does it matter if you're in debt?" she asked. "Everyone has debt. You should get them the things they want."

I thought that I was doing a good job teaching them that debt is not a good thing, and that it's important to live within your means. Wanting a new toy or video game is fine, but it should be a goal that you save for, not an impulse that you put on the credit card.

Money is often a tough topic for single parents. Being in debt is stressful, and adds an additional worry to all of the other items on your full plate.

I cannot stress this enough – Do not go into debt buying holiday gifts!

You might think this is easier said than done. I'm sure there are many people you normally buy gifts for, and you certainly want to get them something nice. How could you possibly afford all of the presents, without having to use a credit card?

There are just three things you need to do, in order to avoid overspending during the holidays:

- Don't buy gifts for all the adults in your family!
- Set spending limits!
- Save early!

Don't Buy Gifts for the Adults in Your Family

At some point in time, you can tell your brothers, sisters, aunts, uncles, cousins, and even your parents, that you don't think everyone needs to buy everyone else a Christmas gift. Do we really need more gift cards? We just all end up spending more money than we want to, and stressing out over what to get everyone. It's not necessary!

The beauty of the holiday season is spending time with the people we love. That doesn't have to cost anything.

I know many families who will put everyone's names in a hat, and each person draws one name. That's who you'll buy a gift for, and no one else.

Or, a really fun gift giving tradition is holding a White Elephant Exchange. Everyone brings one wrapped gift to the get-together. Usually a spending limit is set; thirty dollars is a popular amount. It's not too much, but you can still buy something pretty nice for thirty dollars. The first person chooses one of the gifts and opens it. The next person chooses a gift to open, or they can take one that has already been opened by someone else! It's really a lot of fun, and a great way to spend time with your family.

Set Spending Limits

We all want to buy great presents for our kids. They know exactly what they want; they've seen countless ads about the new electronic gadget that everyone will have. But we have to be realistic, right? We really don't have to spend $1,000 on each kid, every Christmas! You know that your kids are going to get gifts from their grandparents and their other parent. They won't be deprived.

The expectations that many children have regarding what they think they should receive is often unreasonable. They're conditioned by the media and by all of the advertisements they are constantly bombarded with. As a parent, it's extremely important that you set a more realistic expectation for your kids.

Set a spending limit for each child. This will certainly vary among families; it could be $50 for each child, or it could be $200. The limit is up to you. You probably don't want to share the amount with younger children, but if you have older kids, let them know! It's always appropriate to start teaching your kids how much things cost, and how not everything is affordable.

Now, if there is an item that your kiddo has her heart set on, but is more expensive than the limit you've set, there may be a solution. When my youngest son was ten, he was already a Lego master. He found all the pieces of his big brother's Millennium Falcon Lego set, and put it back together. He was on a mission! He hunted for the instructions, and put together every Lego set that he could find in the house. There were quite a few, and they were distributed among many shoeboxes.

That Christmas, my son really wanted the Lego Death Star. It was the Death Star that was still under construction, so one side was only partially complete. It consisted of over 3,000 pieces. The recommended age for this thing was 16 and up; but my ten-year-old was dying to put it together. The price tag was a little over $200.

He understood that my spending limit for his Christmas gift was $100. He also understood that I needed to stick to that limit; making an exception was not an option. But that didn't stop us! We knew that multiple family members would be sending him gifts. There were two sets of grandparents, several aunts and uncles, and his father. So, we sent each of those individuals a photo of my son surrounded by his recent Lego creations, and a request that instead of gifts, his family send him money that would go toward the purchase of the prized Death Star. Think of it as Christmas Crowdfunding.

It worked beautifully! He received exactly what he wanted, and the gift-givers didn't have to stress about whether or not he would like the gifts they chose. It was truly a win-win!

Save Early!

I remember when I was a young mom, the credit union I belonged to had a Christmas Club. This is simply a short-term savings account that can be opened with a very small deposit. I contributed to this account throughout the year, to make sure that I had money to buy gifts at the holidays.

Christmas Clubs are still around today, but you'll find them more frequently at credit unions, and not so much at banks. Even if you don't have a Christmas Club available at your financial institution, you can easily start one yourself!

I'm a big fan of using envelopes for many purposes. If you're not familiar with the envelope system, the concept is simple. Every time you get paid, and create a written budget, you'll include a certain number of envelopes. Each envelope is labeled as a spending category. For example, you might have an envelope for groceries, eating out, entertainment, babysitter, gifts, pet needs, etc. You will actually withdraw enough cash to stuff those envelopes with a designated amount of money.

I've always had a Christmas envelope, and I always will. I have three children, and when they were younger they all understood that they would receive $100 for Christmas. This could be in the form of gifts, or cash; it was up to them. So, every time I got paid (twice each month) I added $20 to my Christmas envelope. $480 was more than enough to buy gifts for my kids! With the remaining $180, I made sure that I got a tree, maybe some new decorations, and one or two gifts for close friends.

Saving for the holiday season throughout the year ensures that you'll be able to avoid at least one of the common stresses that the holidays could possibly bring.

Your Christmas Budget

Determine how much money you can allocate to your Christmas envelope every time you get paid.

$10

$20

$25

$30

$40

$50

Your Giving List

This Person Gets a Gift...   That Will Cost This Much.

Enjoy!

When a single parent is with his or her children, that parent needs to be ON! No one else will step in and give you a break. When you're home with your kids and you get sick, you still need to be on. It doesn't matter if your head is pounding or you're running a fever of 102 degrees. Which, by the way, is much harder for an adult to deal with than a two-year-old. Why can a little one with a fever still be full of energy? I've never understood that.

But when you're the one who can barely stand up, who's going to take care of the kids? You are, of course. You'll make sure they have food, clean clothes (or clean enough), and that they make it to school on time.

You know what I mean; we've all been there. When you're a single parent, you do it all. There are many parents in the group that I lead here in North Texas who have moved here from another state. Not only is the other parent not around to help much, there isn't even a grandma or grandpa around to babysit once in a while.

So, as a single parent, it actually might be nice to have a little break once in a while. Because I know that no matter what you're doing, no matter where you are, you are thinking about what your kids are doing. When you're at work, attending meetings and creating PowerPoints, when the clock hits 2:45 your spidey senses start tingling. You think to yourself, "Ok, John is getting on the bus now, and Susan is staying late for tutoring. She should be home just a little before I am."

We all think this way! No matter what else is going on at work or in our personal lives, we are constantly thinking about our kids, too.

Ellie is an account manager for a worldwide distribution company. She has two little boys—Jacob is nine, and Sam is seven. She's a very busy woman; she's also a very lucky one. Ellie and her ex, Jack, actually get along pretty well. They've been divorced for almost five years, and they both really try to put the needs of the boys before their own. They attend school events, parent/teacher conferences, and Jacob's basketball games together.

When the holiday season rolls around, they're both very accommodating and easy to work with.

"Oh, your Aunt Joanie is coming in from out of town?" asks Ellie. "Of course, the boys can spend the night of Christmas Eve. I'm sure she'd love to see them opening gifts from Santa. I can see them that afternoon."

It's gone on like that ever since they split; Ellie would spend Christmas Eve doing some last minute shopping and making about four different kinds of cookie dough. She and the boys would make the cookies on Christmas Day.

If Ellie or Jack need to swap Christmas Eve for Christmas Day, it's never been a big deal. They've always been very conscientious about making sure that they would all have the family time that they asked for.

But this year, Jack had a different request. His grandfather would be visiting from a neighboring state and he just celebrated his ninety-first birthday. He had only met the boys one time, when they were much younger. This could very well be the last time they would have the chance to spend time together. Jack asked Ellie if the boys could spend four days with him; Christmas Eve, Christmas Day, and the days before and after.

Ellie had to think about that. She had never spent that amount of time away from her sons at Christmas. She didn't want to be without them; but she certainly understood Jack's request. They had been so young when they had last seen their great-grandfather, that they had no memory of him. This would provide the opportunity for them to create some lasting memories. She didn't want to deprive anyone of this chance.

Ellie agreed. Which, of course, brought up a new question—What in the world was she going to do by herself for four days?

Single parents who work full time and are involved in their children's education and extracurricular activities have very little time to themselves. This isn't news, but it's something we need to remember when we do have time without our children. Ellie has a unique opportunity to do something just for herself during this time!

Even though it's during the holidays when she'd prefer to have her kids with her, she can still make some very special memories. One option is spending time with her parents. It would be a completely different dynamic to be there without her children. Maybe she could pretend to be a child again!

You could spend this opportunity doing something you love to do, or doing nothing at all. How many chances so single parents get the chance to do nothing? Not many!!

Adjust your attitude. Turn this into an opportunity to do something just for you! Read books, watch movies, go for some long runs, spend time with your friends, eat at a restaurant that your kids would never want to go to. Do something FUN!

My Favorite Things

_____
_____
_____
_____
_____
_____
_____
_____
_____
_____
_____
_____
_____
_____
_____
_____
_____
_____

Filling the Void — Give Back

Sandra is lucky. She and her ex-husband have a very amicable relationship. They both do their best to put the needs of their children first. They understand how important both parents are in a child's life.

They regularly attend their kids' sporting events, band concerts, and parent-teacher conferences together. They were always willing to compromise and work together when it came to schedule changes. Sandra didn't mind picking up the kids if her ex had to work late, and he did the same for her.

So, when Sandra's ex asked her if he could take their children to visit his parents over the Christmas holidays, even though she was supposed to have them for Christmas Eve that year, she said it would be okay.

Sandra knew that her ex's parents were getting older, like we all do, and his dad was not in the best health. She wanted the kids to be able to spend some time with their grandparents that they would remember for the rest of their lives.

Sandra's own parents lived close by, and the kids are able to spend quite a bit of time with them. When her kids spent time with their grandparents, she could easily see how happy they all were.

Children who are able to spend time with their grandparents benefit in many ways. One study by Cornell University stated that as many as nine out of ten adult grandchildren feel their grandparents influenced their values and behaviors. Grandparents transmit to their grandchildren the values and norms of social order.

Grandparents have the wisdom that a lifetime of experience has given them. They love playing with their grandchildren, introducing them to their friends, and of course, buying them presents.

Sandra did not want to deprive her kids of getting to know their other grandparents better. It meant they would be gone for an entire week, but she knew it was the best for everyone. She and the kids would be able to have their own celebration when they returned.

The only question in her mind was, "What will I do with myself for a whole week?"

She had the whole week off from work, because she typically planned to take her annual vacation at that time of the year. So, while Sandra had no problem letting her kids take a trip with their dad, she really wasn't sure what she was going to do all by herself for a whole week at home!

Sandra considered herself to be a strong, independent woman. She never put herself in the role of victim. She understood that her happiness came from within, and that it was up to her to create a joyful, fulfilling life.

Growing up, her parents were always involved with their community. Her mom volunteered at her school, even after Sandra graduated. Her dad was always helping with gardening projects around their town, and organizing food drives for the local food pantry.

Sandra had loved helping non-profit organizations, but life as a working, single mother didn't allow her to have much time for giving back.

She always felt deep satisfaction by doing volunteer work within her community. She knew that when she spent a Saturday afternoon stocking shelves at their local food pantry, those efforts directly benefitted the town where she, her family, and her friends lived.

The more she thought about it, the more she liked the idea of doing some work for a non-profit during her time without her kids. It sounded like the perfect way to stay busy, and do something important.

If you are looking for a way to stay busy, and not feel lonely during the time that your children are not with you, helping a non-profit organization is an excellent way to spend some time. The people you help will appreciate you more than you'll know.

If you're wondering where you can volunteer your time, just do a quick Internet search for non-profit organizations in your area. Are you an animal lover? Your local shelter would love to meet you. Is there a museum in your town? You could volunteer by telling kids about certain exhibits.

Contact the organization that interests you several weeks before you plan to volunteer. Most of these organizations will perform a background check before allowing a new person to volunteer.

One type of volunteer opportunity that is close to my heart is visiting with Alzheimer's patients at a memory care facility. These state-of-the-art facilities provide excellent care to memory patients. The patients are thrilled to have someone to talk to, or to play cards with for a little while.

Whatever you're passionate about, you can find an opportunity to use that passion to help others in your community. Giving back is incredibly fulfilling. Use some of the spare time that you have helping people.

How would you like to help your community?

_____

_____

_____

_____

_____

_____

_____

_____

_____

_____

_____

_____

_____

ABOUT THE AUTHOR

Diane Windsor is passionate about helping single parents. She is the leader of Single Side Up, the largest single parent support group in North Texas. She has three children, two Boxers, and is married to her best friend.